Neutral Receding Lines

also by j.d.tulloch

Undiscovered Paladins: Westward Rhymes Revisited
(39 West Press 2015)

Hypnotizing Lines: Road Rhymes, Volume One
(39 West Press 2011)

The Will to Resist: and psalms of anger, love & humanity
(39 West Press 2010)

edited by j.d.tulloch

Desolate Country: We the Poets, United, Against Trump
(39 West Press 2017)

Prompts! A Spontaneous Anthology
(39 West Press 2016)

Neutral Receding Lines
Road Rhymes, Volume Two

j.d.tulloch

39 WEST
PRESS

39 WEST PRESS
Kansas City, MO
www.39WestPress.com

39 WEST
P R E S S

Copyright © 2013 by j.d.tulloch

All rights reserved. No part of this book may be reproduced, scanned, or distributed in any printed or electronic form, including information storage and retrieval systems, without permission. Please do not participate in or encourage piracy of copyrighted materials in violation of the author's rights. Please purchase only authorized editions.

First Edition: February 2013

ISBN: 978-0-615-76981-3

Library of Congress Control Number: 2013933064

This book is a work of fiction. Names, characters, places, dates, and incidents are products of the author's imagination, or are used fictitiously, satirically, or as parody. Any resemblance to actual persons, living or dead, business establishments, events, or locales is entirely coincidental.

10 9 8 7 6 5 4 3 2

Design, Layout, Front Cover Photo: j.d.tulloch

39WP-06A

CONTENTS

Volume Two

OVERTURE
PRNDL: Transmission	5

ACT I
In Kansas City ... No, No, No	7
In America Sunday ... and Christmas	8
New Year's Hope ...	10
Pilot Season	11
OK!	13
Clovis First	15
In Red Rock, New Mexico ... a Truck Stop	18
vegas (next	20
In Las Vegas ... with 4 Hours	23

ENTR'ACTE 1
Motets in A	25

ACT II
In Santa Monica ... Mirrored Sunset	27
Wannabes	28
In Los Angeles ... January Outlook	30
A Hollywood Rhyme	31
Stars in the Background	32
Meet Me	34
TheY	35
Hollywood Allure	36
Beverly Center Empty—	37
Dirty Dirty Echo Park	38
Somnolent Stars	39
Bernie the Homeless Guy	40
A Scene at Griffith Park	41
Mirrored Sunset (Reprise)	42
Pilot Season (Reprise)	43

ENTR'ACTE 2
    Motets in B Minor   45

ACT III
    An Airplane Adieu   47
    In Kansas City ... Dropped Passes   48
)e-m-o-H(too: sleepless blues   50
    Innocence: Gone   51
    Three Six-Word Novels   52
    In Kansas ... Taming Lions   53
    Vanishing   54
    Up to Whom?   55
    Southwest Chief   56

ENTR'ACTE 3
    Motets in C   59

ACT IV
    In Las Vegas ... Awake   61
    Dream to Sleep   63
    Govern or? (the con of sin)   64
    The Feast   66
    Leftovers   67
    The Discarded Queen   68
    A Lonely Haiku   69
    Noodled   70
    Bad Music   71
    Remember the Children   72
    Hell No   73
    The ~~Myth~~ Meth of Change   74
    A New Day   75
    Awake (Reprise)   76
    Innocence: Gone (Reprise)   77

FINALE
    PRNDL: Neutral Receding Lines   79

Volume Two

"Man is born free; and everywhere he is in chains.
One thinks himself the master of others,
and still remains a greater slave than they."

Jean-Jacques Rousseau
du Contract Social (1754)

OVERTURE

PRNDL: Transmission

Reverse is a mostly overrated gear except when
backing out of a car Park
a destructive relationship or
a pile of shit

i don't trust those who travel backwards to
recapture a parallel past
relive a bygone present or
recreate a reminiscent future

                                                  (repeat, regress)

back to the places they've already been
back to the places they've already been

moving forward in Drive and letting
what's behind me
what's passed by me or
what's passed me by
stay a rearview mirror reflection of
Neutral receding lines
in *The Lincoln's* back window is
all that i trust is
all that i need

but before losing the only forward gear
that propels me in Low past
who i was and toward
who i will become
i'm gonna need a new transmission

                                              (or rhetorical strategy)

ACT I

In Kansas City ... No, No, No

in kansas city
the lord of misrule ambles   (amuck)
        near imaginary X-mas friends

        dancing wisdom
with sugar plum visions
        clouding heads   (stuck)

in a chimney like the savior of humanity
        like the melting ice cube   (fused)
to the bottom of my empty bourbon glass

dumfounded you ask,
        WHO'S NOT EMBRACING
THE TRUE MEANING OF CHRIST-MAS?   (yes, jesus)

betrayed by his favorite disciple   (rudolph)
crucified in the flue   (expired)
paramedics prophesy a replete recovery   (in three days)

we can visit a mall   (shopping)
sit on his lap   (praying)
beg for what we need   (sowing)
        our selfish seeds of greed ...

and if i
    you
    we believe
        a seat in the artic for all   (eternity)

In America Sunday ... and Christmas

in America Sunday is
the day of the Lord or
the day of football and
freedom is choosing
which god to praise

when i was a kid
clad in my finest suit
to church i went
on Sunday morning
with my mom and dad
until the minister proclaimed:

GOD CREATED AIDS TO KILL ALL THE FAGS

and the congregation cheered
to which i walked out
but we were leaving early anyway
to go to the football game that day
so it wasn't much of a statement

now today
to home i went
on Christmas Day
with my mom and dad
gathered around
the TV watching football
and after a touchdown
the fans in the stands cheered
until the referee proclaimed:

UNSPORTSMANLIKE CONDUCT—
ONLY ONE MAN IS PERMITTED TO JUMP INTO THE STANDS

and fans in the stands booed & hissed
to which the football men
congregated in the endzone
on their knees and prayed
a thank you to an aloof god
for that great play

WAIT!

why are any men allowed to jump into the stands?

AND (more importantly)

why is ~~praying~~ on your knees ~~the key to win?~~
     fellatio   a damnable sin?

because
in America today is
the day of Jesus' birth or
the day of football and
Freedom is choosing
which god to praise

so with their kids
clad in their finest suits
to church they went
on Christmas Day
until the minister proclaimed:

GOD CREATED MARRIAGE FOR ONE MAN AND ONE WOMAN

and the congregation cheered
to which some walked out
but they were leaving early anyway
to go to the football game that day
so it wasn't much of a statement

My New Year's Hope ...

that we
conquer the calendar's control
of our lives ...

that we
embrace
(not waste) Time ...

that we
cherish each moment
of our lives as if it were our last ...

that we
open our consciousness
to a transcendent thought inciting

selflessness
over
narcissism,

charity
over
greed,

peace
over
war ...

that we
(simply)
LOVE.

Pilot Season

i'm headed to Los Angeles
with a
television guest star
who has a SAG card and
too few IMDB credits
two to be exact
to his name

i've been told that
it's pilot season
where landing a recurring role
on a shitty sitcom is
an especially welcomed fate
for the
indie recording artist slash
television guest star

i'm not worried
that we have no place to stay

it's pilot season

and some of his Hollywood
guest star "*friends*"
have said we can
crash with them

i'm sure it will be fine but
i'm packing my tent and
i'm packing my sleeping bag (just in case) and
i'm packing my—

    mostly his stuff
    into *The Lincoln's* trunk

it's huge:

    the amount of his stuff
    (and *The Lincoln's* trunk)

gangster types obviously
selected the Town Car for
the sheer amount of dead and/or live
—i've pegged it at eleven—
bodies that could be
stashed easily in there
or
clothes-cases
shoe-cases
guitar-cases
vinyl-record-cases
desktop-computer-cases
and
just-cases
full of every kind of
fashion accessory known
to (and for) the
heterosexual hipster effete emo indie recording artist slash
television guest star
with a SAG card and
too few IMDB credits
two to be exact
to his name

i'm still not sure where to stow
my dirty underwear

but i'm not worried
it's pilot season

OK!

following the rain
plain wind sweeps me
from magic lantern dreams
to sweet smelling places
where they say there's
PLENTY OF ROOM TO SWING A ROPE
(i.e., swing from a rope)

Oklahoma OK!

Okay Hammerstein
between Huck Finn's drag adventure
and Anse Bundren's newfound bride
one-hundred forty-seven swung

now dope
Okay methamphetamine
is the lynching rope
cinching its citizens' hope

YIP-I-O-EE-AY
Oklahoma OK!

where (remember) useless from diamonds
resided during his drop out days
like his old man before him
(a cook of one kind or the next)

where (remember) the television guest star
resided during his collegiate days
like his old man before him
(a rook of one kind or the next)

each planting his waving wheat

this soon will come into play
—not the missionary flingthing
   but the holy roller thingthing
     which might be one in the samething—

if i can escape a second
(like i did the first)
stuck in Neil Young choruses
(and the toxic fumes from
Amarillo on US 60 West to
in and around
Hereford, Friona, Bovina, Cattle Slaughter, Tex-ass)
all the way to
the New Mexican border
where a lazy hawk
makes circles in the skies
far above the stench
of the melting carrion
slowly burning its way
through the cornea
of my own two
cloudy brown eyes

YIP-I-O-EE-AY
i shall say

take a look
at OK!
L-A-H-O-M-A

take a look
old men
i shall say

they've gone
about as fur as they c'n go
and are rolling home
to where you were

Clovis First

on elm street
tonite far from
the tracks and
twice stuck arms tucked
away in his
suburban nest awaiting
our arrival the
Wesleyan-holiness
minister (and his family)
dislocated from
the Midwest
to save the lost
lambs drifting
to sleep perhaps
to dream in Clovis
first and above the
rest (his family and)
the minister
sit protected in his
safe haven
safe from but
still amidst and
surrounded
by an inherited
dope-dependent and
starving congregation
segregated below
the poverty
line outside the green
zone far from
the blossoming
apple pear cherry trees
of life and the knowledge
of good and evil freely
growing in his back yard:

fruit which he will provide
provided
you put down the needle and
pick up his

safe inside these
walls far from
the tracks and
thrice stuck arms tucked
away in his
suburban nest awaiting
our arrival the
minister (and his family)
guarantees the security of
a warm bed and hot meal for tonite:
fruit which he will provide
provided
we mainline a prayer beseeching his
lord god almighty who
shed some blood for us to
guide us through and guard us from
the debauchery that lies ahead on
the dark streets of West Hollywood

but what the minister doesn't know is
that my veins are already full
(that my cup already runneth over)
and what the minister doesn't get is
that my lite already shines brite from this
bed-room in his
safe haven burning
loudly in the nite etching
a guiding path for the living
dead who sorrowfully wait on this
sleepy life to end
and dream of the next to begin
while another lifeless piece of fruit
quietly in the nite falls from his

apple pear cherry tree of life
while another lifeless piece of fruit
quietly in the nite falls from his
wagon onto the floor

and in the morning i shall arise and wave goodbye
and apprise (t)his lord god almighty that i am
(no thanks to him) alive

In Red Rock, New Mexico ... a Truck Stop

another appears, a portly fellow, and
takes a seat in the booth next to mine.
like the others, he seems detached

(and tired) and void of any expression
of the slightest sign of happiness.
we exchange glances. my nod of

approval (and quick smile) goes
unreturned. another appears, a
television guest star, and takes a seat

in the booth across from mine.
like the others, lunch—mine: burnt
black coffee & an overripe banana—is

interrupted by a pre-recorded public
address announcement: SHOWER
CUSTOMER 102, YOUR SHOWER IS NOW

READY. PLEASE PROCEED TO SHOWER 14.
we exchange glances. our nods of
approval (and quick smiles) shift

from amused to horrified as our
eyes in chorus dart for the nearest
exit. but upon reflection, much to my

surprise, i surmised that not another
soul flinched, nor head turned, as
each blank face, unphased by this

rather unusual declaration, calmly ate
from their plates (and sipped from
their cups) as if nothing strange had

transpired ... save the portly fellow
seated next to me who promptly
deserted his meal (and paid his bill)

before swiftly departing the diner,
smiling and clutching a Hello Kitty
beach towel firmly in his hand.

VEGAS (NEXT

black canyon resigns its sovereignty over
the dark night, abdicating to the colossal
unincorporated lights scorching the valley below.

our accession into paradise
will not
be met with the same raucous enthusiasm
that greets an impending bachelor party;

nor will
our accession into paradise
be met with the same guileless eagerness
that greets a retired baby boomer couple
carrying two comp tickets to *cirque du
soleil: the beatles love* ... however

our arrival in vegas (next
exit summerlin) will usher
in a passionate welcome
to the suburban nest of my
dear friend (and attorney)
[it is a necessity
to have access to good representation
in Las Vegas, even if you are just
passing through: the cops here
have greedy trigger fingers
(like slot machine whittlers)
and they're never more than a few
seconds away from parlaying a simple
traffic stop into a major civil rights
violation: NO OFFICER; YOU DO NOT HAVE
PERMISSION TO SEARCH MY VEHICLE.]
who has already, first, informed me
(and then the television guest star),
followed by an unnecessary apology,

that she did not bother to clean (or
tidy) her home in preparation of our arrival ...

it's not that she didn't want to;
it's that she didn't feel the need to
or (more than likely) just didn't care to ...
i mean, i don't care.
why would i care?
why should anyone care?
(the television guest star)
but that's not the point—
i'm just thankful

that the godlessheathenatheism
encompassing her safe haven
prohibits the proselytization of
junkies tweakers stoners rollers pharmers cokeheads
(many of whom are her clients,
who she saves not because she has to
but because it is the right thing to do)
or any such traveling vagabonds,
myself included, searching for a hot
meal and warm bed for the night:
chili.
chili it is ... again.

the same fruit the
wesleyan-holiness minister blessed us with
last night:
a convenient meal to keep warm
on the stovetop if you do not know the
time in which your visitors may arrive ...

that sounds somewhat biblical
(prophetic in fact)

and on that i do say ...
christians and atheists alike

can agree
(should agree)
that the key
to righteousness lies not in
witnessing your version of Truth
to non-believing naysayers but in
sharing a gracious bowl of chili
with a starving soul in dire need ...

provided
it is provided with
no attached strings
of compliance and
no ulterior motives
of entrapment: *NO MINISTER; YOU DO NOT HAVE PERMISSION
TO SEARCH MY SOUL (OR PRAY FOR MY FATE)
JUST FOR GIVING ME A MEAL AND A BED FOR THE NIGHT.*

no, you take the bed tonight.
i shall sleep on the couch.

that way, in the morning, i
can arise and hug my friend
goodbye, plant a kiss on her
cheek, not as a sign of
betrayal, but as an act of
love, and apprise her sexy
non-judeo-christian-god-believing
(or-is-it-fearing?) mind that i

am grateful she
escaped Bucyrus
(or was it
Clovis first?)
and is now
(thank the universe) alive.

In Las Vegas ... with 4 Hours

If you find yourself in Las Vegas with four hours to kill, then you should:

A. watch Francis Ford Copolla's splendid 1980 edit of Abel Gance's 1927 silent masterpiece, *Napoléon*.

B. listen to the Metropolitan Opera's 2003 performance of Hector Berlioz's 1858 epic opera, *Les Troyens*, while hiking through scenic Red Rock Canyon.

C. march in protest from the Place de la République on the Right Bank of the River Seine, cross the river, and head up the Boulevard St Michel to Place Denfert-Rochereau as if it were 13 May 1968 and you were in Paris, France ... not retrogressing in front of *Paris Las Vegas*.

D. veg in front of your overpriced MacBook Pro, like hipster wannabes, watching brain-cell-killing YouTube videos until its battery dies or your spirit succumbs, which by the way happen simultaneously.

E. pop a Cialis and try in your mind to relive last night's Strip club exploits while waiting for your dick to go limp or eyes to go blind, whichever comes first ... or simultaneously if you're lucky.

F. drive ~~straight~~ forthwith to Santa Monica, bypassing black-topped boulevards and a blast of smog's L.A. lament in favor of shores of sand and a puff of winter's salt-water aria accompanying Helios' hymn of crescendoing solar steeds steering Sol safely from Phaëton's ill-fated finale to Oceanus' omnipresent overture ... since nothing else in the universe matters till sunrise.

The correct answer is F.

ENTR'ACTE 1

Motets in A

1
The simple lessons in life
that we learn from each other
are far worth the price of admission.

2
Patience is waiting for the dough to rise
and then sharing baked loaves of wisdom
with those around you, not bogarting …

    … what was i saying?

3
There are two kinds
of people in the world:

those who live vicariously,
reenacting others' stories

    and

those who live existentially,
creating stories for others to reenact.

ACT II

In Santa Monica ... Mirrored Sunset

Treat with great skepticism
the TV guest star who

(while sitting on the beach)
misses the beauty

of an ocean sunset
in that he was too busy

preening in a mirror.

Echo cried;
Narcissus died;

and I'm standing
fearful of

those who gaze
but can't see

IT.

Wannabes

1
Each afternoon,
hipster filmmakers
depart their parents' homes

(like grease moths
exiting the cocoon in
search of light or sugar),

ritualistically assemble
in Sherman Oaks coffee
houses with overpriced
Macbook Pros in tow, and
pretend to write the next
box office hit, gathering
not for their own benefit
but to the detriment of others:

for only we can see
the prominence of
their shared delusion.

Hiding behind his
Warby Parker Feltons,
which do not Jack
Kerouac a man make,
one myopic with no
imagination—they all
have little or no vision
or (in)sight—declares:

*Ya gotta have a lot of money
if ya wanna do anything too crazy.*

Then I laughed.

2
Each night,
I ritualistically park *The
Lincoln* on a residential
street in West Hollywood and
securely lock the doors and
wait for the auto headlights
to dim before turning away.

But tonight, at 2:07 a.m., snugged
comfortably in my overpriced bed at
Chateau Marmont, I awoke from that
nightmare, untangled my left arm
from the steering wheel and my
right foot from the brake pedal,
reclined myself a bit more, and
declared over and over again to
the half-awake television guest star
occupying the seat next to mine:

YOU CAN'T DO ANYTHING TOO
CRAZY WITHOUT A LOT OF MONEY.

Then I laughed ...

grateful of my prescription
—an overabundance of imagination
and determination compounded with
intolerable eyesight of foresight
or inoperable 20/20 vision—
and tried to fall back asleep
in *The Lincoln's* cozy front seat,
counting not sheep but the seven
hundred twenty-two deeply
deceased Washingtons
(and one IMDB credit)
that I currently have to my name.

In Los Angeles ... January Outlook

today's Times unexpectedly
shot the forecast
into my eye:

70 & sunny ...
with an
80% chance of

                s   m   o   g

left with no other choice
to the Hollywood Hills
i went for a hike

and upon reaching
cloud's rest promptly
rolled & lit a cigarette

        then pondered why it's
        illegal to smoke
        tobacco
inside]
        but
        legal to burn
        fossil fuels
                ]outside

        when again Downtown Los Angeles sighed

before gasping and exhaling
some more carbon die-ox-ide*
into the atmosphere

Carbon dioxide is the primary gas emitted through the combustion of fossil fuels. Since the start of the Industrial Revolution around 1750, human activities have added carbon dioxide and other heat-trapping gases to the atmosphere, which in turn have contributed substantially to climate change and caused Earth's surface temperature to rise.

A Hollywood Rhyme

at rush hour, SAG seeking
shirtless studs insolently
step all over Satchmo
wishing upon a star (not

his) and weave through
crowds of star seeking
sightseers hoping to be
discovered: a morning jog.

despite condemnation
from television guest stars
(*KEEP MOVING*), i stop and
gaze at the supernova

encompassing Grauman's
Chinese and ingest the
pungent ersatz of fried
soylent green papayas

or tomatoes or hornets or
lanterns on the boulevard
everything's gone green: a
pending premiere. this

recipe does not bemuse as
the cacophonous touch of
fame to my sole reiterates
why i came: not for fame

but to remind that fate is
unkind when your dreams
only exist within the confines
of a classic Disney rhyme.

Stars in the Background

Each week,
hundreds of anonymous migrants
exit the bus agog
and fill the great hall in Burbank,
chasing stardom's call.

Their virgin faces mugshot
and provident forms measured
for a mere twenty-five,*
but no one here's rejected
regardless of shape, age, color, creed, or size.

Once the forms are filed
registration heralds
the paltriness of their rapidly razed given names
(no matter if it's Pitt, Longoria, or ~~Wayne~~ Morrison):
the *actors*' reward invisibility
with wretched hours
and minimum wages of the same.

But when the inexorable chasing ends
and stardom finally rings
with a role cast in stone
and typed neatly on a call sheet
under the simulacrum
of atmosphere and standins,
the ticket has been dispensed
on this cursory track to imminent fame.

And when the camera rolls
(and action declared),
each walking stereotype
(or cinematic wallflower),
with faith unseen
by any priest monk or nun,

proudly chants
(with unparalleled conviction)
the extra's mantra
beckoning infamy's reign:

it's better to be seen
briefly crossing the background
in a motion picture scene
than it is not to be seen
as a minute flashing blip
on the gawking talent scout's
ever changing radar screen.

In May 2011, the Los Angeles City Attorney's Office, citing the 2009 Krekorian Talent Scam Prevention Act, informed Central Casting that the company risked prosecution unless it stopped charging photo-registration fees. While denying that it was subject to this law, Central Casting immediately stopped charging performers seeking background work.

Meet Me

prowling
the grove
in hunt of
a 200 dollar
pair of jeans
an unknown
television guest star
delicately sips
a stiff caramel macchiato
from Starbuck's
with the symmetry
of a ballerina

at home
in his natural habitat.
swigging
a two dollar black coffee
from Bob's
a fledgling
screen writer
cavorts
upon a flimsy
metal and wood chair
absorbing
the stage

in the penumbra
of the clock tower.
a presage solicits
passersby to
meet me
at Third and Fairfax

my apple fritter
nearly consumed.

TheY

the sauna at The Y
where even

the Village People
dreaded to tread

beguiles
real estate brokers

prepping for a hard day
of swapping plots

for the haughty
naked eyeballs penetrate

bare backed Clydesdales
galloping erect

muscles pumped
winning L.A.'s clash

with self-image
a-part in the shower

i eschew
TheY

Hollywood Allure

        t
        h
        i
        s
        m
        o
        r
        ni
        ng
    i awoke and the zipper
<on my sleeping bag was broke>
<(n) dog hair and pot seeds>
<carelessly cultivated on the floor>
<of the apartment of the two>
<stoners who provided shelter last>
<night i was covered by the>
<morning light blasting through>
<the sliding glass balcony door i>
<spotted a stack of 45s sitting idly>
<atop a spindle stabbing the sky>
<with tone poems of color that>
<resonate from the subterranean>
<chamber of the concrete bunker>
<in the house that Nat built>

and
thus the allure of my Hollywood
                                   reality

Beverly Center: Empty—

the middle of the day
in they go
emptyhanded

hours later
out they come
emptyhearted

hushed voices
narrate the tale
shrieking wordless

logoed paper bags
the only witness
lewdly advertise

taste and waste
remunerated by
parking slips' validation

sought but unreturned
ardor prostrates
crumbled and forsaken

on the garage floor

Dirty Dirty Echo Park

the ancient bard
staggers sunset

from pub to pub
his dirty prose
echoes about the park

past the groucho Marxist
disposed on the corner
left bleeding by the skirmish
enriching himself and
ameliorating for right

maladroit cops and
wing-ed pies
grace Edendale
when Hollywood seizes
reign o'er the silver screen
stealing bathing beauties
swimming in shorts

supplanted by features
talkies take hold
of box office receipts
giving the slip to
anarchist communes

trust-funded hipsters
strut sunset
from pub to pub

infecting the park
their clothes dirty

Somnolent Stars

tonite on Yucca and Wilcox
the stars fall brightly

in the hallway
a lambasted
drag queen slumbers

outside Ed Wood's door

window ledges
typecast
unengaged street walkers

in chinos

Willie the Pimp
angles the porch
leasing doxies

for a twenty spot

a rapacious trick
bludgeons to sleep
the Fernwood Flasher

in a meretricious cage

hostages of fame
sanitize the narrative
of Hollywood disgrace

at the transubstantiated Lido
a television guest star comatose in the closet

Bernie the Homeless Guy

at two a homeless man
patrols the quixotic boundary
between Beverly Hills and West Hollywood

with the audacity
of a border patrol agent
on the Mexican line

he'll tunnel you
under the Center
from San Vincente to La Cienga

for some company
and a pack of smokes
he announces me

to a coterie of *aspiring* writers
languishing outside the Coronet
pretentious fucks fleeing

LIVE
NUDE
GIRLS GIRLS GIRLS

bread squandered
on a phony rack
modest Bernie reeling

ALIVE
BARE
POCKETS POCKETS

tracks my scent to Norms
his breakfast lurks
on the counter

A Scene at Griffith Park

                                        FADE IN:
EXT. GRIFFITH PARK - DAY

A TELEVISION GUEST STAR effortlessly hikes a trail on Mount Hollywood. A WRITER and a FORMER GAME SHOW CONTESTANT, both attired in improper footwear, follow behind, unhurried. The Television Guest Star pays little attention to his languishing companions.

> TELEVISION GUEST STAR
> Fucking pansies!

At mountain's summit, the Television Guest Star abruptly removes his shirt, revealing a six-pack of abdominal muscles. He catwalks on the lawn in front of Griffith Observatory, unaware of his surroundings, hoping, however, that others are aware of him. Moments later, the Writer and the Former Game Show Contestant arrive at entertainment industry's zenith, energized.

> TELEVISION GUEST STAR (CONT'D)
> All right, bros. Let's head back down.

Hungry, the Television Guest Star and the Former Game Show Contestant promptly descend the trail back down the hill, deserting the curious Writer. Replete, the Writer sojourns, digesting the aesthetic of his morning production:

A great dome coruscates in the unseasonably warm Los Angeles sun. Downtown reclines shrouded in linens of silken smog in the concrete basin below. Hollywood's most iconic lettered landmark juts unembarrassed from the hillside of puny Mount Lee. Snow caps *telegraph* peaks frolicking from Ontario to Cucamonga.

The Writer muses on the lawn in front of the observatory, aware.

                                        FADE TO BLACK.

Mirrored Sunset (Reprise)

Sunday in Santa Monica
north of the pier
the wind recalls howling dead

the hushed Santa Ana wind
resurrects departed Afghan sand

it cremates precipitated ash and dust
ordered by generals to surround
neurotically lined crosses flank
star spangled draped plastic coffins encase
specters of unknown comrades fallen

a mirror image of Arlington
sheds its sepulcher for the west

[impotent to prevent eradication
a gulf away unwitting soldiers
engage for Middle East sovereignty]

Sunday in Santa Monica
south of the pier
the wind dismisses howling dead

the rabid Santa Ana wind
embalms lingering Mohave sand

it occupies chiseled muscle beach
ordered by talent agents to battle
stable swinging ropes clutch
cold steel barrels strengthen
armies of unrelenting Hollywood hopefuls

a mirror image of Tinseltown
dips its silhouette in the sunset

Pilot Season (Reprise)

with the final trophy dispensed
and red carpet rolled up

for yet another year
Hollywood frames its consideration

from honoring its bright stars
from casting its fresh faces

to regaling full of hubris
in its impending summer season

no one steps out of line
in the shadow of Disney's castle

wannabe hipsters pretend to write
and an extra perfects his entrance

leaving casting couches on the floor
homeless souls do plot their exits

while an unknown TV guest star
approaches a thousand Facebook likes

the Hollywood allure dissolves to memory
in the mercy of the night

ENTR'ACTE 2

Motets in B Minor

1
Sometimes
less is more,

and

sometimes
enough is too much.

2
Preaching to the choir
falls upon deaf ears

as does trying to communicate
with a narcissist
who is consumed
by the pursuit of fame.

3
Never trust a thespian
who wants to spend
his last four dollars on hair dye.

ACT III

An Airplane Adieu

the libidinous blonde
decorates the aisle

with a short skirt
fresh off the rack.

she sits next to me.

her ringless finger
(and dreaded hair)

shimmers sunlight
beaming through

cabin's portal,
recalling Medusa.

petrified, i revisit Foucault and *Folie et déraison*
while she studies magic bras in *Glamour*.

i suspect we have little in common.

In Kansas City ... Dropped Passes

in March
the concrete tundra
forages
on discarded
Christmas tree carrion:
        i arrive

disrupting
latent lives
with moxie alive
until freedom's bell rings
at midnight:
        the girlfriend

projecting
absentee fatherism
onto the one
with whom she's
chosen to make a life:
        the boyfriend

consoling
the unruly hysterics
of an insecure partner
who manipulates
with an oxymoron of control:
        the writer

transcribing
dime store dramas
and flaccidly participating
but somehow
actively affecting:
        sleep

in beds
borrowed and created
by shenanigans
reeling in
daily re-re-re-inforcement:
      energy wasted

on rent control [prepaid]
that progresses on cruise control [idle]
whilst regressing idols roar
passed lives
past passengers wailing a pass hailing Marys:
      a drop.

I N C O M P L E T E

)e-m-o-H(too: sleepless blues

                                                                          Home—

       a place to rest your
head a pillow a warm
sack the backseat of a
car the bitterseat of a
bus train or plane the sleeping
bag on the floor of a stranger's
apartment the inflatable
mattress on the floor of your parent's
office the hammock in your sister's
backyard the futon in your friend's
closet the unfamiliar bed of a
hotel motel or hostel the
tent pitched inches above high tide on a
beach under that lofty star a sunny waxing
moon envisions approaching fantasies loitering with
       guitar in hand a tune:

       i've got the space-heated attic
masquerading as my own crib air-matress on the
floorsleeping middle of the night body achin' calf
crampin' eyes wide open hot as fuck dehydrated
       sleepless blues

       and one thing's for certain:
       all that lead me—*(w)here?*

Innocence: Gone

ice white pellets furiously
pelt transparent glass sheets,

embedding veracity.
wind chimes ring and

sing insomniac dirges.
newspapers ricochet and

dance in dissonant rhythm.
deaf ears slumber

in winter's hibernation.
innocence erased by daylight's

cleansing blades: purity gone.
home. anon.

Three Six-Word Novels

1
Published a book;
　the people ignored.

2
Justin Bieber shat;
　the people rejoiced.

3
Freedom fled;
　the people were silent.

In Kansas ... Taming Lions

suburban clone
of downtown pub
smells circus

poser hipsters in
flat-brimmed hats
cowboy hats

stocking caps
fedoras
compete in

three rings
singing
pop-corn culture dirges

masculinity compromised
by a pacifist FAGGOT
an Iraq vet clowns antagonistically

walking a tightrope
between sanity
and madness

the ringmaster
choreographs
enlistees to the grave

VANISHING

deposited securely
in the zippered front pocket
of his sullied winter coat

thirty-eight dollars
(the day's
panhandling crop

harvested
on urban soil)
banks on asylum

from ne'er-do-wells
Ron absconds
on his red bicycle

exiting the transient stage
his taillight twinkles
on and off and

back on again
before vanishing
in the chasm of dolor

Up to Whom?

With help seizing the night
It seemed (at the time)

A good idea drinking
A bottle of generic NiteTime.

Under the influenza of
Self-induced twilight dreams …

Reality floated by my bed room depot
Without a seat to spare.

Under the influenza of
Self-induced twilight dreams …

Fantasy floated by my bed room depot
With some change to spare.

Tomorrow?
Up to me. Up to you. Up to us.

Southwest Chief

Brass buttons guides cushion riders
to vacant seats in dark glass cars.

Westman highballs outta Paris des Plaines,
amblin' to Sin City along the glory road.
À plus tard: Kansas City.

My grip: a guitarless case awaiting axe's
acoustic reunion, despite being drafted
into transporting a cappella garb
transferred from forsaken portmanteau.

[One thinks Spielberg might (not) be: proud.]

I think. In
harmonies conjugated, missing backseat
Lincolns traded for circus living.

Therefore I
Am. Be. In
melodies transposed, matrixing dreams
of inner automorphism: G.

A blickering, flinking lite
divides)separates(unites
coach to lounge car connector cables
screech like tired play grounds camped for rest.
Door slides open for a mere peak before
unplugged apparitions stagger through: shut.

Tunes expire in early retirement.

A psychedelic vision gone
waiting on turns to chase bandits
from car to car atop of train: A.

Tunes expire in early retirement.

An auditory hallucination here
strutting a furry baby or a fat
cat's stray notes till the spun
wheel wins: perorating reverie.

Still no sign of Boxcar Willie,
the Boxcar Children,
or my stolen music.

Colorado kidnaps mysteriously
vanished passengers, save the
snoring lumberjack seated across the aisle.

High iron atop
the Sangre de Christo Mountains
past the semaphore signals of Ratón, now Glorieta Pass.

Jesusless crosses carry good news,
transforming current/electrifying crowds
from valley's abyss to Golgotha's zenith.

In the dining car,
I'm sandwiched between
a Jewish defector (from the former Soviet bloc)
and a Muslim French/Italian tourist (from Algeria).
A fight over the same
genocidal god ensues

when there are so many other
non-genocidal gods
from which to choose.

ENTR'ACTE 3

Motets in C

1
Find meaning in the world
(and in those around you)
by acting selflessly

rather than

acting selfishly
by using the world
(and others)

for your own gain.

2
We only have so many days
and each one spent wasted
is one less lost in a haze.

3
Why spend your entire life
cultivating a dying garden

when beyond the white picket fence
is a flowering pasture waiting to be explored?

ACT IV

In Vegas ... Awake

the balding suit throws money
at the fake-boobed Ukrainian

bartendress as the hopeful
gamer inserts cash into the

slot. no winners here. on
television, Laird Hamilton

paddle surfs past the sound of
the Great Oz proclaiming his

magnificence. crashing waves
prevail. Stella quenches my

thirst as an imaginary
longboard carries my mind

from destinations known
back to worlds of fantasy

envisioned only in locked-door
dreams. a scream. uninvited

alarm's inconvenient reminder
spoils sanity. crashing sound

waves return reality, sending
subtle signals to hourglass

sands. time. slipping. sliding.
falling. gravity prevails. a lift?

with tips, the laws of physics
defied. the balding suit left

stiff. cock but no tail.
foreboding clouds abduct the

day's last moments. Westwind
yields not as Thor descends

unrestrained on the valley.
rain. departed zephyr spawns

an eerie, harmonious calm.
city slumbers. silence survives.

darkness reigns, savoring each
second until sunlight usurps.

first rays creek in window cracks,
signaling insomnia's sway over

Sin City's sleepless shadows.
Sin City's sleepless shadows.

tick tock.
tick tock.

restless desert residents desert rest.
awake.

DREAM TO SLEEP

every
    (w)here
       here
    (t)here   vegas *frightens*

s t r u   n   g   o   u   t clones^{clones}
sur—flatbilled—round
new era (dog tags)
t it d un d
 w se t r e
slightly ri
     g
     h
    t d
      a
     n
      g
       l   a l i
        e   e   n
        starbucks d g
        safe caffeine
        (atthesamerateas)
        amphetamine.

the doctor says the doctor says the doctor doctor says says:
ARE YOU ARE YOU CLEAN? HOW 'BOUT SOME BENZODIAZEPINE?

xanax **screams**
to
adderall junkies |=++++++++++++++++=> fixated
                     on gaming machines
dream   [perhaps]
to
sleep.

Govern or? (The Con of Sin)

Immobile again.
Lacking inspiration.
Deliberation
without motivation.
Absent.
Transient.
Tiny motion?
A prosaic location?
Can fix this fragment.

In Madison
the Nightwatchman descends
raging against the machine.
Worlds away
the Optimator
taps out.
Wonder Twins
try to entice
incite wagers.

Sanguine stakes
pledging parlays
for a lay.
An ante of assets
for some ass.
Senses stimulated
on a long shot.
Fickled fate
in a money shot.

Bet Makers
miss the Mark
treading heavily
on rocks of ice.
Melting.

Evaporating
like pensions.
Funds dissolving.
Derivatives decapitating.

Headless unions
rally.
Sway.
Say.
ParLay.

2day
workers reunite.
Incite what's right.
Write hisherstory
lines of unison
undone by governors.

Govern or?
We! Us! U$!
E-gypped.

Wes(t) falls for the
con of
sin
when
Lib-E-A.

Again.
I sit.
Immoblie.

Absent.

The Feast

```
            HUNGRY
            U
HUMANS      G
            R
            Y
            T
            H
FOCUSED     E
      N     M
            S
            E
            L
            V     O
            D E S C E N D
            S
RED               Q
  O               U
CASINO  BUFFET
K                 U
            L I K E
                  S
            D
VULTURES
            M
            A
            N
            DAILY
            I
CARRION
            G

[LUNCH]
```

LEFTOVERS

desperation cloaks hope's silent cry—

a frail woman wearing years beyond her age
(and an *I LOVE LAS VEGAS* baseball cap)
sifts silently through trash bin scraps ...

moments later, she joyfully emerges
with a half-full can of beer
(abandoned by an inebriated tourist)
and without hesitation chugs it.

desperation cloaks hope's silent cry—

a frail woman wearing years beyond her age
(and an *I LOVE LAS VEGAS* novelty tee)
sits motionless in a scooter of mobility
embracing a square placard: *DISABLED VETERAN NEEDS HELP* ...

moments later, she graciously accepts
a half-eaten bean burrito
(gifted by a well-intentioned tourist)
and without hesitation grubs it.

desperation cloaks hope's silent cry—

Fremont Street's victims feed on leftovers:
strangers' discarded American Dreams.

situation: bleak.

The Discarded Queen

snugged safely
in Summerlin's security

streetlights quiver
(off and on)

a half-moon away
day abdicates

to night
on The Strip

an old queen
pushes

through calm
Tropicana water

awaiting arrival
of today's trendy trade:

twenty-ones
(engaging in

egregious gossip)
espy only themselves

steaming
the discarded queen

(wrinkled and worn)
dealt no more

A Lonely Haiku

buried in desert
sand, a seashell missing the
sea waits to be heard

Noodled

misplaced palm trees sanguinely map
boulevards from City Center to seaside sand.
the trail delivers me beach's end, where

revealed in Red Rock Canyon's glands only
oceanless desert sand. unwilling to succumb
to disappointment's oblong cry, i hastily grab

my zipperless—and favorite stick—and blindly
charge a swelling dune as if it were the last
wave. but its stoic disregard for my mere

presence graciously repays by launching me
orbitsville. my flimsy fuselage eats it at the
foot of Keystone Thrust, leaving me noodled.

Bad Music

bass sounds box in stereotypes
sharing smoky secrets.

synthetic cymbals click,
invading elusive cliques.

escape?
no. it's the place.

beer bust bracelets bring bottomless beverages,
save top-shelf spirits.

born this way, a genderfuck lip-syncs stale pop,
selling drag show shots for dollar tips.

[fuck you fake Lady Gaga.
i liked you better when you were Madonna.]

a sole hipster shows himself,
rescinds a single.

tip sent & intended
for a stiff Scotch.

bartender repents;
dead president kept.

straight into slots,
games control

like brokeback
down lows

cloistering
life away.

Remember the Children

when losing money in Vegas
you never think of the children

but the croupier who deals you a nine when you need an ace
and watches intently as the plastic cocktail waitress
distributes sycophantic libations until you are way overserved

that nameless gaming industry worker
(in all likelihood)
has a kid

who attends a public school employing a strict dress code
despite the fact that
many of its students' mothers earn a living wearing no clothes

flailing their naked bodies around a pole
despite the fact that
the law prohibits hanging a garage sale flier from one

and in Vegas when you hire a hooker
remember how that job seeker is classified by local authorities—
as a laborer who engages in commercial sex for exploitation

and that nameless sex industry worker
(in all likelihood)
has a kid

so when losing money in Vegas
remember the children

Hell No

Las Vegas bachelor parties birth a testosterone fueled mob mentality: mass hysteria driven by one d-bag's quest for snatch and ridden by the rest. Drunken drunkies [fifteen in number]

descend straight on Stratosphere's Cirque du Soleil-like show, vampire style, sucking a Bite. Sapphire's strippers in sight. Bellicose blue-balled-stags rambunctiously board the White

Whale carrying a license for lewdness that surfaces inside seedy strip shows, seducing shitfaced suckers. Destination: The Luxor. New York & L.A. *partiers* represent Jersey. Soundtrack:

Springsteen. Born in the USA blasts. Blown speakers crack. Bachelors all tonight. Rings hidden. Bands of commitment gone. Idol wannabes' song. Cinderella's limos at midnight arrive to

drive those still alive to *glory days* [now night] filled with bimbos whose poles arouse trolls. For our reality show contestants still rolling on molly, four hours of *exotic* dancing doesn't satisfy.

It's on to Déjà vu Showgirls, where live titties are the second coming ... coming ... cumming ... oh ... oh ... oh ... oooooooooh! Save it for a cold shower tomorrow when sober sanity squeals,

Hell no.

The ~~Myth~~ Meth of Change

sphinx sits atop
watchtower
spying friday night.

vegas in
lock down town up town
a riddle guarded sits watch.

jonesing tweakers' giant pupils
wander nervously through
sin city's bloodshot eye socket,

darting and pacing
the pavement
for change:

hope
don't
pay

[the rent]

spent on
the meth of
the masses.

a pocketful
of change
remains.

promised change
elusive as
promised lands:

gritting teeth in desert sands.

A New Day

at dawn
Casino Center
bus stop
brings out
a cast of
characters unseen
in one's daily stream:
a recovering
crack addict
whose wife
chooses rock
over life.

pipe replaced by can
(brown paper bag in hand)

Jamal says
he can
no longer watch
his lover
turn backroom tricks
for her next dirty fix.

transit on approach,
roach nearly toked

my new friend
bumps my fist
(bus token in hand)
and rides away,
gliding on
Vegas hope:

a new day.

Awake (Reprise)

chasing melodies unwritten
from Spring's mountains
to Fremont's experience,

the new day bestows
its inglorious promise:
a sacred pledge.

adventure marshals in
orange clad
case numbers.

bracelets contain
chain
restrain.

freedom revoked by
addiction's
choke hold.

a trap?
a choice?
a reminder.

daydreams resuscitate
ephemeral arias of retroinspection
but soon secede

to nightdreams
transposing fantasia's locks
into keys of rhapsody.

tick tock. tick tock.
restless desert residents desert rest.
awake.

Innocence: Gone (Reprise)

some write about
birds & trees & leaves & bees &

greet the day with innocent hymns
of backyard suburban sweet.

some write about
the street.

the beat
of beats passed.

the past realism
of a generation

in action
not without

imagination

but partaking
transcendent

surrealism
enabling

creation
in existentialism:

purity gone.

FINALE

PRNDL: Neutral Receding Lines

Pages turn,
Recede, into the penumbra of anamnesis, yet
Neutral lines linger,
Departed from their homes,
Lost, between your hands and heart.

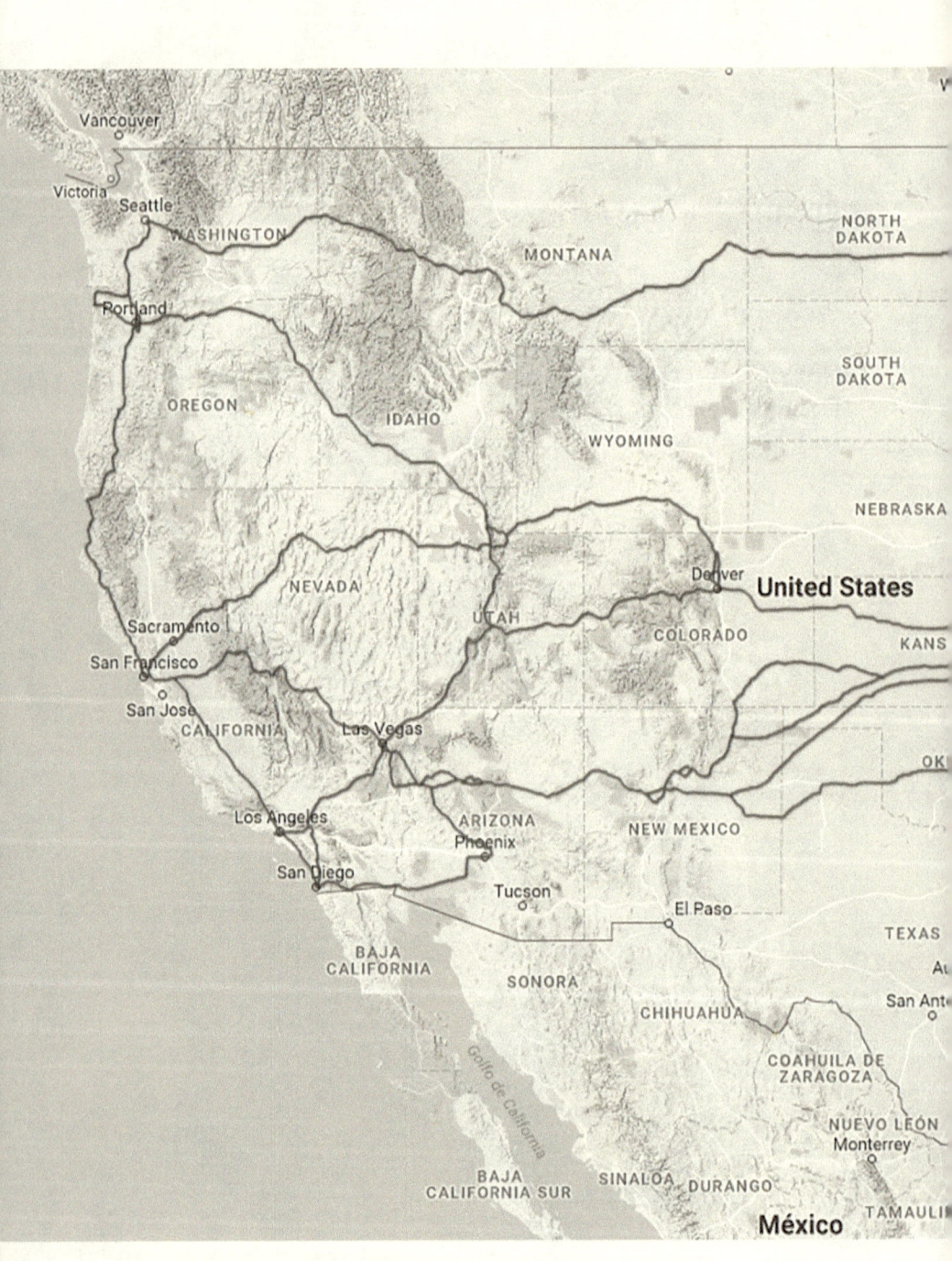

August 2010 — February 2013

j.d.tulloch is a writer, filmmaker, and social activist. He is the founder of 39 West Press and has worked in broadcast radio and for the management team of the late Godfather of Soul, James Brown.

www.ingramcontent.com/pod-product-compliance
Lightning Source LLC
Chambersburg PA
CBHW021958290426
44108CB00012B/1125